Still • Life

Also by Robert Vas Dias:

The Counted
Thanking You for the Book on Building Birdfeeders
Ode
Speech Acts & Happenings
Making Faces
Time Exposures
Poems Beginning: 'The World'
The Guts of Shadows
Leaping Down to Earth
The Lascaux Variations

As Editor
Inside Outer Space: New Poems of the Space Age

ROBERT VAS DIAS

Still · Life

and Other Poems of Art and Artifice

For Elaine Feinstein
in admiration
and in friendship,
affectionately,

[signature]
13 Nov. 2010

Shearsman Books
Exeter

Published in the United Kingdom in 2010 by
Shearsman Books Ltd
58 Velwell Road
Exeter
EX4 4LD

ISBN 978-1-84861-121-4
First Edition

Acknowledgements

See page 134–135.

CONTENTS

For Maggie

Preface

Still · Life because, a late morning flâneur on the streets of Paris in 1979, and wandering by accident into the Galerie Berggruen, I became intrigued by meticulously incised etchings of multitudinous arrangements of jugs, bottles, vases and pitchers, and I didn't get the point. Why devote all this energy to making pictures that didn't seem to be about anything? I went out, had a coffee, and came back. Something kept me looking. They had an edgy mysteriousness, they were provocatively ambiguous, strangely compelling. I was bemused by their apparent representational intent, but they went beyond the representational, they were more like abstracts. Back in London I got hold of books and catalogues on Giorgio Morandi, found that he'd said, "Nothing is more surreal, and nothing more abstract than reality."*

That opened up for me what I'd thought at first a problematic practice, and it also led to my becoming aware in my poetry that a preoccupation with ordinary things—their *thingness*—is not simply with "things exactly as they are" but as they are transformed by the imagination and reconstituted in art—recycled, as it were. Things are meaningful and seductive as the material for a poetry of the quotidian, as things were for the Dutch masters, for Chardin; as *bodegón* (things of the pantry) were for Zurbarán, Meléndez—the painters of *nature morte*. "Still" may imply "dead" but the painting glows with a vibrancy that lasts beyond its making, it is alive in the way assembled things affect and change each other, the way they project themselves and all around them in the play of light and shadow, colour and texture, weight and volume. It was very much as an organic, *living* construct that those "representations" appeared to me.

The title of the series of poems from *Select Things* in this book (see *Acknowledgements*) occurred to me as a result of seeing Patrick Caulfield's show at the Hayward in 1999. The ironic tone of the paintings, their celebration of banal décor and spurious exclusivity—one of the paintings is titled "Selected Grapes", 1981, and a print is called "Paris Separates," after the wording that appears on a shop awning—brought to mind "select" to modify "things" that are the opposite of exclusive, that are mundane, ordinary, undercutting the temptation to give them a special sort of status or fashionability. Nevertheless they are desirable, they mustn't be thrown away but require that they be recycled, that something be made of them. Jugs, vases, pitchers, bottles … as well as envelopes that can be posted again, plastic containers, elastic bands—I throw away very little of anything, to the chagrin of my long-suffering wife. But what is involved in the making of poetry if not the reconstitution of words to "make it new"?

---

* In Italian: "altro ritengo che non vi sia nulla di più surreale, e di più astratto del reale." In explanation of what he meant, Morandi went on: "I believe that what we see is the creation, the invention of the artist, if he is capable of removing the diaphragms, the conventional images, which superimpose themselves between the artist and things." Interview recorded on April 25, 1957 by the Voice of America, as quoted by Renato Miracco, "Nothing Is More Abstract Than Reality," in *Morandi 1890–1964,* ed. Maria Cristina Bandera and Renato Miracco. Milan, Skira, 2008, p.295.

STILL LIFE

Arrangement is all:
        how everything falls
                into its place, the inevitable
                        space that's been made
                                to receive it

making room so
        space is relinquished
                as the tern flashes into it
                        and out sequentially
                                so I cannot see

the exchange but only the line
        of flight: the secret
                of still life is knowing
                        where that line is
                                continued in the mind's

eye before it arrives
        as the bird makes
                instantaneous adjustments
                        to follow a picture it has
                                of its perch bounded in space.

SPEAK TO ME SILENTLY: STILL LIFE AND POETRY
A WORK-IN-PROGRESS

The Secret Starer
Observe still life intently for long periods of time without fearing ridicule, embarrassment, intimidation, hostility.

Steady scrutiniser, private
ogler, look-kissed and caressed,

getting to know, hold,
fondle, thus acquainted

with grief, with joy,
warmth, the abundant arcs,

curves of the human shape
in its changing, seen in what

we make and shape: *stay me
with flagons*, arabesques of arms,

luscious handle undulation,
pout of jug-spout.

Composing Objects
A retro gestalt

Air: circulates invisible billows
of breath-and-colour-rhythms

that demarcate the object,
animates its stillness.

If you're depicting something made
by human beings, that seems to me

to be enough. It does describe people:
four retro dining chairs, with

moulded plastic seats, arranged around
a square café table, a raffia-wrapped

bottle of chianti, three olives,
an empty glass on top. The people,

the people left a moment ago but
bars of sickly pink and brown

light and shadow slanting across
the space betray their joyless

after-hours conviviality, the room
empty and waiting for customers.

Natura abhorret a vacuo

Arrange things how you will
randomly, or obsessively

they will insinuate their inimitable
nous, alone or nestling

in proximity to others
as the single restive word I *am*

agglutinates into other
dimensions I come

to occupy: *we* together is more
than the sum of one and one.

Iron to Air, Air to Iron
    Still life as monument to the Industrial Age

I would make of the iron jib crane—
Armstrong Mitchell, Newcastle, 1883—

a rhythm of its black triangles, staves
resonating in sapphire-still air above

Venice's pale turquoise harbour water;
it is famously still, silently

rusting on its ornamental brick casement,
redundant in the Arsenale,

a relic that raised great guns into
naval turrets, but see! it saturates

the space it dominates, stridently
decaying into resonant stillness.

Origin of the Jug
    Journey to the maker

Joanna's mermaid painted
on the knobbly little jug

has pendulous breasts,
an ample belly and where

the scales begin, a large haunch
as befits a great fish whose tail

rises from the waves clear
around the other side of the jug:

who would have known that
halfway up the Cambrian hill

from Llanbrynmair you
could glimpse through trees

the far-off sea just before
the pottery where husband

Michael threw the pots
and cups and jugs she decorated

her eye's mind no doubt
on that myth-frequented sea?

Nature morte
> *Three artists in the eighteenth-century present*

Apples, peaches, pears, grapes
sink into a mound of furry pulp in

Taylor-Wood's time-lapse video 'Still Life'—
what happens clear enough—but also

the glistening pomegranates,
apples, azaroles, and grapes in a landscape

in the varnished still-life oil
by Meléndez. It always needs saying:

composing the present ripeness
is the closest we get to the eternal,

a basket of fruit forever ripe, the painted
promise, still, of *the four Seasons*

*...the aim of composing a cabinet of foods
of every kind produced by our favourable clime.*

I live only streets away from Julia
who etches architectonic geometries,

patterns we inhabit and see around us
in the fabricated still, and always unstill, life.

Decomposition is the undying end
since everything will consume everything.

Two After Morandi
His sleight-of-hand

(1) Natura Morta

The sky, well, not the sky, the wall
then, is golden, the sun, no,

the light, hazing the objects
on the grey ground, well, a table

more like a dusty plain, the
objects familiar, though not, are

conjured into brown importance
as features on the little stage

of the brown room, his brain
that contains them, makes

the space in the landscape
that contains me, not me.

(2) The In and the Out of It

Two lidded flagons stand, pillars
to the portal of a grand precinct

part-hidden in shadow within.
I'm outside a minster of utensils,

mendicant on the plain looking in.
What do I expect to gain, what boon?

Do I think I'll be invited in to gawp
amongst great bottle-towers,

colonnades of vases, a town
on a strange tableland whose inhabitants

glide black-cloaked in anonymity
in a conurbation of familiar shapes

where I, the unfamiliar solitary wanderer
hammer at the gates of horn?

My order is not your order

Suppose he sees his wife's head
as an angular oblong, her hair
a wavy brown strip down one side,
purply curly horizontal strands on top.

One eye's (much larger) above the other
which appears to have an oblique
hat brim shading it, but no
shadow, her mouth and lips are straight

lines, a rectangular *ahhh*. She has
a quizzical, intent look, she looks
intelligent, she must have been
a looker. I never met her.

She's his idea. He took things, people
as they are and made them up
into his view of people, things, picturing
them so you could rearrange

the world, try it out with the strange eyes
of someone else which is always a good idea
when you're hung up on someone
else's order of the universe.

The world may be in a crazy mess, you think,
but odd perspective is all, the way things
line up, or don't, and from his perspective
everything about her fell into place.

THE MEETING

I like to find
what's not found
at once, but lies

within something of another
nature,
in repose, distinct.
Denise Levertov, "Pleasures"

For Maggie

Simply: glass and crockery arranged
        on a table in the sunlight or

not, shapes that flow
        into one another, simply or not,

each establishing its own
        space but then quite

quietly changing it
        for the other: I'm talking

still life, motionless, life-
        less though it's still *life*

embracing the other
        as my lips embrace

the cup, your lips
        folding over the lip …

we cannot meet like this
        we cannot help but meet

at all, all is unstill and folds
into the moment slowly

the curve that surrounds
everything, jug, cup
bottle, bowl, you and me.

Nature Morte

A coastline is no such thing of course,
but from where I stand the distant
strand's a line between the colour planes
jostling in the heat-haze against the ultramarine-
cobalt sea and the tree dark where I rest
after sun's daze:
                                an arrangement of vases
segmented on the table of day's span.

Pausing at the nominal view, I see
I've misapprehended the parts, imposed
on the scene my own rhythms—tiredness,
buoyancy—and do not notice where,
seamlessly, one blues's laid in over white
and scraped away and light brushed in
so it fills and forms the floating space and makes
this life lie still for an instant, composed.

—

THE LASCAUX VARIATIONS: FRACTALS OF BEING

Really, the interior is an extension of still lifes,
I mean they are interchangeable.
                    — Patrick Caulfield

Where one thing ends
          and the other begins
                    is the no-man's land

my inquiring eye
          scans for movement
                    flicks over your face

in shadows, the space behind
          or within your eye, what
                    you're thinking, the face

betrays or else a fake
          depiction, a 'picture'
                    of dissembling joy or melancholy

the languishing catastrophes,
          details of this or that passion
                    spasms of the self with another

that have edge but no ending
          over time but a continuous
                    meld in time

of shapes of colour and light,
          each limb and look, your features
                    changing with the fleeting

recollection of taste and smell and gesture
        in the times between one view
                and another: the one that is now

being the one we see, and yet
        what we imagine to be,
                as if we didn't know.

2

Where one things ends
        and the other begins
                is the no man's land

where my gathering eye
        flicks to complete
                animal shapes on the rock-face

painted aeons ago in shadow
        in flickering light
                and copied meticulously

underground in a cave
        that is not a cave
                in depictions that are pictures

of pictures of running bodies
        animals which are still
                and forever running

towards a space that flows
        with imagined images of flight
                and the chase. All moves

in the still environment
        of re-imagining, a fake
                depiction, a 'picture'

of how animals and men leapt
        or stood for an instant,
                still: the ones that are now

being the ones we see, and yet
        what we imagine to be,
                as if we didn't know.

3

Where one thing ends
        and the other begins
                is the no-man's land

where we imagine beings
        and objects delineating space.
                Today you're not

in the room with me as
        this jug of roses
                makes the colour-beginning

illuminating the dark interior
        with their brilliant insistence, forming
                an eidolon of love and loss:

nothing is there, always, until something is
        made of it, *nothing is more surreal,*
                nothing more abstract than reality,

as those who made the paintings
        knew, who filled the imagination
                with recreations of what they saw

being the ones we see, and yet
        what we imagine to be,
                as if we didn't know.

4

Where one thing ends
        and the other begins
                is the no-man's land

where a line is not a line
        despite Klee who took it for a walk:
                in no-man's land no one walks

and the line, an artifice, exists to nudge us
        to imagine the figure it encloses
                the borders we draft and draw

that demarcate and separate.
        The line is a useful fake because
                night falls, borders are crossed

in dreams, in candlelight: the makers
        on rickety scaffolds who incised
                these marks thick with mineral pigment

were intimate with artifice
        saw the space in-filled with jostling
                ibex, bison, aurochs, horses

that lines alone could not reveal.
        A place in time can be for
                you and me a resurrection

in art of those who knew their subject,
        played colour against the shapes
                of a subterranean brain,

the one we see and yet
        what we imagine it to be,
                as if we didn't know.

TURNER AT THE CLORE

In the world you climb
an eminence, time

after time you come
upon the littoral willed

of your imagination where
the round tower thrusts

off-centre, or the gaping
gorge draws you

deep and enchanted, land
sky or sea on the coasts of

the dream, literal bourne
you cruise for the colour-

beginning of ecstatic
shipwrecks,
the erotic deluge.

Conjugal Love Poem

What you see is not the way I see.
>What I see is just the ways things are,
>>Everything is always as it seems.

What colour are these trousers?
>You say they're grey, I say they're green,
>>What you see is not the way I see.

Whether blue or black, rough or smooth,
>Against the grain or uniform,
>>Everything is always as it seems.

Let's shelve our books alphabetically.
>No, you say, by size for harmony.
>>What you see is not the way I see.

We've lived together, you and I, for years
>Of harmonious disparity, for
>>Everything is always as it seems,

And that's the way I'd rather have it.
>Let's embrace our incongruity. Or not:
>>What you see is not the way I see.
>>Everything is always as it seems.

Apotheosis of the line:
At the Stanley Spencer Studio Sale

As can be seen from my descriptions of this composition [Hampstead
Heath Litter, *or* The Apotheosis of Hilda] *and indeed from the way
I speak about my pictures, the chief source of feeling in composing
them is* what *is happening in them … ?*
—Stanley Spencer, Letter to Hilda, 1954

Take a line, bend it, extend it,
circumscribe an idea for herding cattle, the line
flows from an arm extended
into the neck of a cow, *what*
is happening, the cow's haunch
becomes the man's arm
on the cow's flank, and the rest of the herd
follows from this:
Cows Being Herded.
Lines enclose cattle shapes
and the man standing, his arms
a guidepost, shouts the lines
and they heave and mass and turn
left at the edge and scuff and stamp
out of the picture.

Take this line into bed,
pa and ma's bed,
*at the time of being a child a great
moment to me, when possibly
because I had not been well
I was in the centre of the bed,*
and they were brought their breakfast;
and make the line imagine the
big black tin decorated tray

with the circles made by the cups and saucers
and the teapot and lid on the circular tray,
and at the foot of the bed the four hillocks
formed by the four sets of toes.
But where is the child, what is happening
in this scene of connubial bliss?—
ma embracing pa, and the tea things
a happening on the landscape of the bed:
Mentally I have been 'bedridden' all my life.
The child is not on the bed.
Stanley's portable easel was a pram.

Make this line move, cross, connect
and reconnect: it is an idea
for figures walking, for a Resurrection,
a Visitation, or *Hampstead Heath Litter*
or *The Apotheosis of Hilda*.
You are everywhere in the line,
you are in the litter which all the figures
are reading as love letters—the litter
is for them alone, each line
a letter telling of absent lovers.
Love litters this place never before made
of paper, scraps meant to be
read and taken up and assembled into
the Great Design of Things.

Carry this line into the kitchen
amongst the pots and pans and Elsie
washing up, ironing, and into
the hospital ward and bathroom where
Stanley and the orderlies scrub floors,
bathe the men, paint them
with iodine, polish the brass taps:

I have done nothing else but scrub
since I have been here.
I think it has done me good.
The line dissolves in the soapsuds
on the floor, becomes the
colour-beginning of the quotidian,
our lives in kitchens, bedrooms and bathrooms,
Stanley's soldiers forever
inspecting kit, making beds, sorting laundry,
performing ablutions:
these are the scraps of a life saved,
squared for transfer to a larger picture,
a part of the world & life of love,
a possible happening in heaven,
all the preliminary ideas and studies
for an interior, or landscape
of the divine ordinary.

EDGAR ALLAN POE AWAKENS IN ISLINGTON

Tap-tap on the roof-
    tiles shudders him
        awake (For the love of God,

Montresor!) immured
    but still breath-
        ing in the catacomb

of the bed, not moving,
    straining to hear
        what he imagines are

                footsteps outside
                on the parapet,
                for pity's sake

rustle of black wings
    beaks tap-tapping
        at their pickings

in the gutters,
        heart's candle guttering
            in the stuttering dawn,

no escape from the brain's
    night-time slammer, and the
        shattered awakening.

CATS AND OTHER HOWLS

Night-time howls in
the back garden: baby?
feral cat? sirens' wail?
in this city of day-and-night
emergencies we can only
guess at but the feral cat
is careful to avoid,
impelled by his own
urgencies and liaisons
with the kill.

Or the overweight tabby
next door unable or unwilling
to use the catflap, who
one day drops in
the open bedroom window
where I discover her
asleep on my pillow?

So: what baby?—or is it police
on their way to a raid, a riot,
a killing on the bus—flowers
tied to the bus stop—
or have they got intelligence
of another sickening
'event' on the Tube,
or is it a 'domestic' to be sorted
by patience and persuasion?

The howling could keep you
perpetually fearful of
muggings, stabbings, bombings, or

else it's just the usual
cats on the tiles, the woman
next door having an orgasm,
the baby crying itself to sleep.

The Wilds of London

Running I must
    tell you this:
        fox on the doormat

outside the front door
    large fox   big brush
        but I didn't tell you:

we looked at each other steadily
    fully two minutes
        neither of us stirring

nor releasing eye contact
    until quietly I
        spoke to him as I would

a dog   *hello boy*   it was
    then he turned
        his mild brown eyes away

in what had to be contempt
    (slid under the neighbour's parked car).
        Of course   felt a fool

betrayed an understanding
    both of us going about
        our business food-gathering

for the family indoors or wherever
    his was in this tarmac and paved-over
        habitat nearby in someone's back garden?

The Square?   Highbury Fields?
        The deserted traffic island copse
            of Highbury Corner?

He'd have to cross the gridlock
        from the Holloway Road
            St. Paul's Road   Canonbury Road

Upper Street   Station Road
        (he'd never make it
            someone's dinner

the reddish smear
        on the zebra crossing didn't
            make it)
someone's dinner
        a series of piercing shrieks in the shrubbery
            behind the back wall   didn't make it

the rat its back broken by the trap
        dragging its hindquarters slowly
            down the road won't

(make it).   WHERE?
        Where is the safe house?
            WHAT shall we have for supper?

Snake and Serpent
For Toby Olson

A week before nearly stepping on a black snake
on the trail in the Cape Cod National Seashore,
I stood before Elihu Vedder's 'The Lair of the Sea Serpent'
at the Boston Art Museum, admiring the fierce expression
on the monster's face at the end of its fifty-foot-long body
coiled in the dunes of what looked remarkably like
the Cape Cod National Seashore, where we are
looking for bleached driftwood twigs half-buried
in the sand, some of which I fancy have features
not unlike Elihu Vedder's mighty sea serpent
only smaller, they might be fossilized
snake babies, unburied by the wind which with
the lightest of archaeological touches brushes
away the sand to reveal the neolithic brood uncoiling
at my feet and scrolling their 'S's in the sand
in the direction of the soon-to-be-enraged mother
who is just now sunning herself behind the dunes.

This takes place as quickly as the black snake flicks
free of my approaching right foot——
a quick charcoal scratch in the white sand——
so that you never see him, even doubt I do
(*In the poem it can be real*, you write later),

but I know, as the painter knows, he is even now
winding toward his lair where,
nestling in the poison ivy, his dam will be
roused to avenging fury, baring her horrible fangs
in the Grand Manner, arousing
'terror and awe' in the Exhibition Rooms,
confounding all sceptics and doubters.

THE LANGUAGE OF ANIMALS

The animals take part in the stories
we tell of rescues, races, Laika's voyage
to outer space, we swim with dolphins,

keep canaries close to us, they
can save us, sing to us, sometimes
macaws and mynah birds talk to us

the animals are part of the stories
they know of chambers, pillows, nests and lairs
the language of unfettered affection

it's not that they're humans in disguise
it's not that he is barking, or she
likes it in the doggy position

the memories of animals are part of our own
elephant memories, goats are horny as he is
and we're all descended … etcetera

the animals are part of the journeys
we make, we'd be lost without them
we feed them and they feed us

dogs and bears dance out our fantasies
cats purr our peccadilloes
and tales of love and faithlessness

the animals are part of our stratagems
to chivvy *duende*, making and knowing
the secret language spoken in dark parts.

DO ANGELS EAT?

After Albrecht Dürer, Melencolia, 1514, engraving

I come down in the morning after a stormy, sleepless night and
here's this angel flopped in my garden like García Márquez's old
angel with enormous wings but this angel is female and she's
not old and she's sitting on the little plinth I was going to put
a potted plant on, she's sitting there with a hang-dog look, not
dejected really, more of a faraway, contemplative expression
as if deep in thought. She doesn't look very happy but maybe
happiness has nothing to do with it, maybe yearning, nostalgia,
regret, an angelic anguish, she's just down, she's certainly down,
ha ha, but I don't feel like laughing. I ask her if she'd like a cup of
tea, would you like a cup of tea? I feel like an idiot, how would
you feel asking an angel if she'd like a cup of tea, do angels eat?
It's said they like manna but I haven't got any, don't even know
what it is, have no idea where to buy it. Her wings seem too
heavy for her, they're certainly large, their tips are trailing on the
ground. She ignores me, she sits there looking rather miserable,
how would you look if your wings suddenly got too heavy and
you had to make a forced landing in a tiny town garden? She has
that blowsy, windblown look. I say, can I help you?—the kind of
question you'd ask an intruder so as not to alarm him, not, what
the hell are you doing here, and then the bar comes out, the
lunge. She acts as if she doesn't hear me, she's somewhere else,
far away, she's inside her head, she includes me out. I'm not part
of her world, angels don't run in the family. Can I help you, I
ask again, gently. Please say something I say, trying not to sound
testy. It's as if I'm speaking another language entirely, no, as if
I haven't spoken at all. What am I to do? Call the police? The
council? How can they help? Take her away? Where? Where does
she belong? She doesn't belong to me, does she. She just happens
to be in my garden, sitting there dejectedly, well, not dejectedly,
just subdued, compelled by something irreconcilable, overcome
by something. Is she sorrowing for our suffering? Maybe she's
working out the alchemy of probabilities. I know: she's trying

to figure how to fly out. It seems an impossibility, she's like a swan in a very small pond, not enough run for lift-off. She's bound to stay here forever, until ... do angels ever die? What will I do with her? If she's here day and night how will I cope? Why has she disturbed my life? How do I reconcile myself to her not answering, not speaking, ignoring me, how do I accept her perched upon the little plinth as though she's perched upon my soul?

CONTEMPLATING THE DEVELOPMENT OF CUBISM FROM AN ALTITUDE OF 32,000 FEET AND AN AIR SPEED OF 625 MILES-PER-HOUR

Ogling her soft geometries
    through the frosty port
        six miles up, puts me in mind of

whirling through the sculpture garden
    of the Kröller-Müller Museum
        near mid-winter closing time, searching

for angles and views of a body
    that seems to be moving, or
        is it me?—circling her

from more than one angle,
    a plane revolving through the floating
        world at rest, now describing

a three-quarter rear section, suggesting
    the beginning of an intention
        to arise, spin out from the span

of seventy-five years when the kinetic charge
    released by Lipchitz leaves me
        his nude about to take her body off.

A Backward Glance at the Past of the Futuristic Present

Look! Rayist vapor trails
        incise zinc white
                lines : inspired

calligraphy etched
        on the fabricated
                cerulean sky-ground.

O Citizens manifestoed
        across the azure by
                divine engines!

We're post-historic.
        Blast anachronistic
                Transports! What's Art

but penetrating
        movement, lines
                of force? Forward!

O limitless design, rays
        of the future projecting
                the blockbuster present!

FORMS OF MOVEMENT

For Tamar Yoseloff

1
Stand before the tensed
metallic, its energy coiled

in seamless ellipses,
imagine her hands still

caressing, forming, polishing,
a tide of energy, moon-force

tirelessly urging wave on wave:
copper coils in tight dynamic

now at rest in the gallery
behind glass walls that curve

above crescent Porthmeor beach,
far rollers forming, gathering

speed and height, coiling
over the wet-suited surfer

forever poised in the instant
gleam before foam-break.

2
The moment's broken.
The crest in-folds the lone

figure—is he carver
or carved?—the kinetic

surge speeding him under
and along its cutting edge

ever closer to the earth-bound
shore, energy seemingly spent.

3
The coppery flow endlessly
seduces, *something still and yet*

*having movement, so very quiet
and yet with a real vitality,* she

said, the hard form in her soft
hands dynamic of the sea

in timeless shifting back and
forth: the day, the work.

4
Then flow, then the slow
recoil, then build-up once

again, and again he's ready
with his body, *I, the sculptor, am*

*the landscape, I am the form
and I am the hollow, the thrust*

and the contour, and then
the beginning: mystery of wave.

March 3rd 2007

Earth's aligned between sun
and moon, time to dream
of coincidence, my hand
in collision with planet
earth and then with a body
hurtling toward me
on the courts and both within
30 days, my hand fractured
twice: that's the astronomic
conjunction all my life has
tended towards so I
mustn't complain must
I, it's a matter of a force
meeting a moving object
which is an immutable
law of motion or some
damn thing or other.

VACATION BLUES
For Michael Heller

He left Point Departure for Lake Paradox
in the Vicarious Mountains where the fish
though eager to take the bait, and plump,
are not succulent. The lake murks
in Deception Valley's bottom
and is reached, after a difficult slither
down muddy Desperation Trail,
via Lost Man Creek. So much
for vacation spots, he mopes,
I should've stayed put, what point
in travelling this far only to stumble
into Ambiguity Cavern, or worse, trip
over the lip of Dead Man's Leap,
which drops you into Abomination Rapids
and then the plunge over Nullity Falls.
This is country life? Better to breathe in
diesel fumes in the Heavenly City,
the rolling armpit of the subway,
the dog mess in Needle Park, at least
you know you're in the State of Grace.

Renault 4

Our old Renault 4—which is sinking up to its lug nuts
behind the piggery, white mould misting its windows,
a lichen-like efflorescence blooming on the dark blue
vinyl seats—has become our own permanent
automobile sculpture garden between the stone
outbuildings of Ballylinch where nature quietly
metamorphoses the fabricated into the organic, where
people might pay to admire the aesthetics of rust,
decomposition of the late twentieth-century
artefact in rustic surroundings.

The sculptor might have titled it "Going Home,"
thinking of its hundred-thousand-mile trip
up and down interminable motorways of boredom,
avenues of déjà vu, streets of small errands,
messages and hotels, back and forth
(Swansea to Cork, Holyhead to Dun Laoghaire,
Fishguard to Rosslare) and ending
as marriages end, leaving recollection
to worry its way into the thin loam
of the steep hillside patch overlooking the sea,
where bindweed pulls at the wheels
and fails to move them, the battery dead,
leads corroded, plugs burnt out.

Plastic in South-West Cork

Caught in brambles, March winds
fray and shred last summer's
black bin liner; in a tree a forever-white
tatter snaps aimlessly signalling what
lost cause, what plea for help or surrender.
Where we fast-walk our four-mile circuit
working up an aerobic sweat, Irish navvies
hacked out the narrow roads
that switchback up and over
hills to reach the farms gouged in
the hillside overlooking
the sea and now-dead villages,
piling up stones for hedgerows
to stave off starving. Now trapped
carrier bags rattle, belly and empty,
and in the ditch a tiny polystyrene
flotilla emigrates, on the way
to the culvert under
the Baltimore-Skibbereen road,
down the bohreen, out to the bay
bound for America.

Plastic Potters Melamine Plate

It established the tacky domestic
decor when money was tight
and infants crawled the floors;
its stylized oriental floral
pattern quickly faded,
and it cracked or failed
to bounce on the kitchen floor,
becoming cat bowls or saucers for
plant pots for a time, surviving
as reminders of former family,
previous trips to the Melmac boutique,
old flats, old injuries, dead pets.

ANGLEPOISE DESK LAMP

large orange bird swivels
its head, casting inquisitive
glances over my desktop
mulch for word morsels,
wriggling phrases, twigs
to potential nest epics,
trails a feathery beam
over leaf and sheaf,
scavenging the midden
she wants me to cull, fling
out somewhere that is not
home, not my own
compost and cache
of seeds he'll crack, break
into song

DIXON ENDURO PENCIL SHARPENER

Impersonal, the 1930s Constructivist sculpture squats
on my shelf, the grinding cogs hidden within
the semi-opaque, brown plastic shavings chamber,
its handle in the upright position, a raised arm
about to drop and execute its unthinkable
act. The iron pillars on either side
have the profile of a turbine apostrophized
by Spender, or early Auden, as the functional
vernacular of power, containing within it
both hope and destruction, emancipation
and exploitation: the better life, and the price to pay
in the wearing down to uselessness.

Brown Teapot

Fool your friends! the ads for dribble cups
in the back of comics promised, but this
is a serious teapot, *short and stout,*
though *tip me up and pour me out*
it puddles tea on the table top
or in my lap, no matter what.

It's not a trick, it's cheap and not
funny, ill-designed, the knob on the lid
too small to be pinched and held
by thumb and forefinger when it's hot
or wet, and the lid slides off and drops
when the teapot's steeply tipped.

When I squint inside I can never tell
if the tea is weak or strong, it all looks brown.
This teapot's the sort of brown that goes
with nothing else in the kitchen,
in the house, or anywhere,
but is purely itself, a brown
that insults taste but forestalls criticism.
It's not a matter of aesthetics,
it rejects aesthetics, it is just matter.
It is not even ugly, the concept of
beauty does not apply, it refuses to be
discussed in such effete terms.

Because we use it twice a day
it's larger than it is, one could say
it assumes a disproportionate
importance—a centuries-old
functional form of the earth shaped

and fired, and which has itself
shaped the nature
of a land, a culture, a people.

If it had a mind of its own
it would tell me to shove it,
this subjective, impressionistic,
pretentious nonsense: wrong.

ESTWING HAMMER

Naming things is only the intention to make things.
—Frank O'Hara, "Memorial Day 1950"

When you have an idea that grips you
as you grip a finely balanced hammer
like an Estwing, and feel not only that just
about any job is possible but that you are
a professional hammer wielder, a man
for whom swinging a hammer rhythmically
comes easily and naturally with just the right
expenditure of energy;

when you have an idea of a structure
beginning to form in your mind
with extraordinary clarity;

when you have what you think is a sound
idea you can build on;

when dreaming of building you feel you know
exactly what you're doing even if
on waking you feel you might not;

when things begin
to fall into place as if held
by invisible nails that sink
into the pores of the wood: you can hear
the ringing rising in pitch as the nails are driven
deeper to join beam to beam.

The house has already risen,
already admitted him into its various rooms,
already changed the landscape forever.

THE GLASS

cannot be called
my own, as this is
our dog, your sweater;
the dog becomes what
we make of her
and talks our language;
the empty sweater
retains you
even picks up on
the dog, but the glass
gives its own shape
for the moment only
to what's inside.

I can see past it,
it has so many views
that it presents
what you will
at any given time,
and says nothing of us:
there is only what enters
us, the interior flow,
accommodating to the usual
channels, the glass
itself a brittle conveyance
of a restless abstraction,
and then it is put away;
it is not of me, not of you,
when you are away
it is an empty ocean
across which your voice
wavers, cracks, shatters

PETOSKEY STONE

This is a speckled fishback world rippling on the sandy lake-bottom near the shore, glistening when I lift it out. Cold and smooth, it contains many small universes within its fossilized egg-shape—polygonal cells, the smaller wedged between the larger, cell edges serrated like sea shells but water-polished and each with a frozen, dark nucleus. Edges, spots, the small universes fade from the heat of my hand, become a speckled dusty grey. I try caressing it to life-semblance, this egg of lifeless molluscs and cold geometries which has emerged from water, motionless in warmth, never to be alive where it lives in my house between seas.

Meditation on a Return Ticket

I pick up my life
and take it away
on a one-way ticket
            — Langston Hughes

I have a return ticket I will never use because East Midlands Trains made me an offer: it was cheaper to buy a return than to pay for just one way. The offer was that I could go somewhere and come back for less than it took to get there. We're talking money, but time, as they say, is money, and so is space: I could go as far again as the distance I covered in the first place. By standing there I'd have gone twice as far, gained more than I lost, arrived before I left, wishes become actualities. In fact there would be nothing to be imagined, no anticipation or fulfilment, no pleasure, no sorrow, all feeling already felt. It would be like being in a railway coach going forever backward into a dark tunnel leading into the terminus.

Langston was getting out of an impossible situation, an impossible South, starting over. If the offer were available would he have bought the return ticket just to fool them into believing he'd return? I think not. If I took them up on their offer I'd be back where I started, as though I'd never set out full of anticipation at the intimate conversation I'd have with you, as though, after our meeting, I had not been changed forever. I did have the impression the season had changed, it was warmer, but perhaps this was a subtle touch by the rail company, the heating system stuck on 'full', windows jammed, aisles full of passengers sweating out the second leg of a return trip. I would have saved money but have to admit that I fell for their marketing ploy, that all trips were round-trips ending where they began, seamless, purposeless except for the fact of travelling up and down fulfilling some marketing manager's hyped-up scheme of a day out on the rails, and not a journey that goes somewhere and ends somewhere else so you can tell someone you have left, you have arrived.

NORMANDY BEACHES 2008

Apart from any other consideration, we are faced with the immense
difficulty, if not the impossibility, of verifying the past. I don't mean
merely years ago, but yesterday, this morning. What took place, what
was the nature of what took place, what happened?

—*Harold Pinter*

Sudden colour swirls of flexifoil
sand kites plunge, thrust, brush-
stroke sky, calligraphy
of late summer messages above
wide sands of Banc de la Madeleine
off the beach they still call Utah.

> *Before me lay the coast and the sea. The*
> *horizon was strewn with hundreds of ships,*
> *and countless landing boats and barges*
> *were moving back and forth between the*
> *ships and the shore, landing troops and*
> *tanks. It was an almost peaceful picture...*
>> Oberstleutnant Friedrich-August, Freiherr von der Heydte,
>> Fallschirmjäger-Regiment 6

Tide's out, afternoon sun less
warm than I thought this mid-September,
surf moderate (it can whip up
a cross-current rip
in storms, shelving sands
shifting, spilling out
the past on the beach).

> *...we could see France miles away. There*
> *was the coast, and to one side of us was*
> *the* Nevada *blasting away with its 14-inch*
> *guns, and in the early dawn it seemed to*

light up the sky every time it let a salvo go.
Pfc. Monico C. Amador, 531st Engineer Shore Regiment, 3rd Army

Half-buried in dunes:
German bunkers, *stützpunkte,* massive
walls pocked and chipped,
rusted iron rebars dangling, yet
the structure insistently indestructable,
Rommel's Atlantic Wall, his
Hauptkampflinie, main battle line,
along the coast between la Madeleine
and les Dunes de Varreville.

*When we were nearing the French coast
the ship that was just ahead of us blew up.
She was loaded with ammunition and
needless to say there were no survivors.*
A.C. Lamey, First Mate, Greta Force

Dark, rank casement chambers
stink of piss, the banked sand
hollowed and hillocked by *Nevada's* shells
from seven miles out to sea
six decades on.

*The ship artillery was the worst, before
the first landing-boats came out, there
was like a wall of fire coming towards us.*
Franz Gockel, German soldier, 352nd Division

She runs down the beach
high-stepping into surf,
and as the waist-high wave laps,
curls over her, she jumps
and throws her arms up,
laughing and shrieking…

It was very difficult to see anything now
for all the sea spray and smoke. There
was a terrific jarring, grating sound
underneath, as though the whole bottom
of the craft was being torn out. We all
lurched forward with the impact. I
gripped my rifle hard.

Reg A. Clarke, Royal Engineers

Beyond breaking wavelets
a surfer flat on his black board
slowly sculls, waiting
for the next promising seventh
to lift him up, bear him beachward.

With orders to go, we got to the beach;
I dropped the landing craft doors...The
German shore batteries were shooting
back at us. We could not believe their
accuracy, we just lived in hope.

Lieutenant Commander A.W. Chappell, RN

Scavenge high-tide's shell debris
on Tare Green and Uncle Red:
they landed in the wrong place
two thousand yards south of where
generals and admirals of Neptune
and Overlord, air recon, meteorologists,
cartographers, tide and current analysts,
French Resistance agents winging
messages via homing pigeons
had reckoned as A-OK.

The sands shift with tides and storms.

We'll start the war from right here.

Brigadier General Theodore Roosevelt, Jr., 4th Infantry Division

The surfer breast-strokes his board
furiously ahead of the just-
breaking wave, pivots
to the crest and is rushed
tipped and tumbling
into foaming shallows.

Soldiers were going straight up the beach.
I saw tremendous courage from the
Americans coming ashore from the
following assault waves. Sadly, many lads
never made dry land...

Lieut. Cmdr. Chappell

A dozen landsailers caroom along the beach
in stiff wind, missing kite flyers,
people walking their dogs, the dogs
yapping and scampering off their leads.

I made my way forward as best I could.
I was hit again, once in the left thigh,
which broke my hip bone...I worked
my way up onto the beach, and staggered
up against a wall, and collapsed there.
The bodies of the other guys washed
ashore, and I was one live body amongst
many of my friends who were dead and,
in many cases, blown to pieces.

Sergeant Thomas Valence, 116th Infantry Regiment

Sand-dune contours
recapitulate half-nude or

half-clothed young women
sunning themselves under
the leeward side of the seawall.

> *It was very—what can I say, well, I*
> *started praying loudly. And tried*
> *through the praying not to think about*
> *what is coming towards us. I just made*
> *these quick prayers.*
>
> Franz Gockel

CODA

Sands shift with tides and storms ...

exhuming a thing foot kicks against
sticking out of the sand, greenish,
caked with hardened, cement-like
sand and small shells, grotesquely
twisted and jagged, heavy for its
six-inch length, metal oxidized
a turquoise green by seawater,
copper-coloured where
the verdigris has worn away:

lethal piece of shrapnel
from dreaded 88mm shore batteries,
shell-casing fragment exploded
from a ship's munitions store
or ejected from an LCT?
American or British or German?

What difference to generations undone,
drowned, run into the sand, or buried
in geometrically laid-out cemeteries,

named on marble crosses, Stars of David
or under *unbekannter, known only to God?*

Sands shift ... uncover the connection
between annihilation and liberation.

> *I saw my first German dead. He must have*
> ~~*been*~~ *killed while running. Even in death*
> *his body seemed to be trying to surge*
> *forward. His helmet and uniform was*
> *all in place. He was wearing glasses, still*
> *not broken. I remember saying self-*
> *consciously to someone, "Well, he won't*
> *bother anyone again." Now I wonder*
> *whether he ever wanted to bother anyone.*
> Captain John C. Ausland, 29th FA Battalion, 4th Infantry Division

The sun's lowering behind the seawall,
swimmers, and surfers toting their boards
leave the water, heading for their towels,
sunbathers cover their nakedness.

THE CRUNCH

What rubbish: dried feathery moss
filaments, compacted lint balls,

lichen-covered bits
of wood, dry sheepshit

and cowpat pieces: in a cunning
meticulously woven basket

of grasses and twigs thick
and thin, plus undifferentiated

debris: one season's jackdaw nest
the chimneysweep reamed out,

put by the front door for fireplaces.
What energy burnt by father, mother

to wedge their fledglings' safehouse
within our home, my love, keeping it

from predators who'd scavenge
and covet and ruthlessly foreclose

on house and home, expenditure's
ruin of the seasons' toil?

DOMESTIC ORDINARY

I'm not making custard, she said, no use
heating up the planet and besides, I'm tired.
Fine, he said, I'll eat it without,
but we're increasing global warming anyway,
he added, with what he thought was restraint,
having just emerged sweltering with the herd
in the tube, reading (trying to) a book made of forests—
by just living and breathing—he explained, thinking
not only of carbon dioxide but the pair of pyjamas
he'd bought that day made wholly of polyester,
and wasn't that stuff made using vast amounts of non-
renewable fossil fuel? and what about the wine
they had poured from glass bottles
the pub across the street throws out by the binful
every week, or the tuna from tins, all manner
of food heat-treated, injected with antibiotics
hydrolysed, extruded, reconstituted, coloured
and shrink-wrapped, brought home in plastic carrier bags
which even now are clogging drains and sewers
and blowing across the desert sands of North Africa
in great tattery eddies which will outlast us
by hundreds of years, which will never go away,
and when will the Great Screw cease its turning,
its energy gradually failing in the implacable entropy
by which everything is used up or runs down,
the precious store every generation has
inherited over aeons, plundered—yet he forebore
to mention any of this and they sat down quietly to eat
their stewed fruit plain, in domestic tranquillity.

THE HANG-GLIDER MAN
For Elke and John

He's the only one who does nothing
    says nothing, stands there perpetually
        in readiness, he has prepared himself

he's ready, he has been ready
    for days, years, centuries
        for this or the next moment when

conditions are right, the instant propitious,
    the light, the weather, the wind,
        especially the wind is

prodigal, when he, a kite at the end
    of an invisible string, can soar,
        slip free, for the moment, of gravity

earth's waiting grave, to float above
    trees, meadows, farms, villages,
        the dark river valley …

From the car his wife shouts, Everyone's getting fed-up
    waiting!—who's driven up here with friends
        on the country road along the cliff-edge.

It's hot, the wind-sock's limp,
    still he stays in his clinging
        insect-wing canopy spread out in the sun

on the dry ground behind him.
    His partner scans the sky and shrugs,
        the road watcher around the bend shouts,

All clear! the contender's fettered in his bindings.
        The friends sweat and fret. How can this da Vinci
            vision of a flying machine sustain him,

how can he stand this tediously drawn-out
        time of waiting for an epiphany? Why
            does the hopeless anticipation

of riding the wind obsess him?
        Can't he fly a kite, build a model airplane?
        Grown men have done less.

What impels him to perform the literal act
        when a metaphorical one would do?
            A thermal wisp of sortileges?

From the car they see nothing divine
        or profane is about to happen,
           see nothing stirring

the leaves, for them
        the time is not now, nor
           will be soon, most likely

never, they cannot feel
        the urgent tug and pull
           of flight buoyed by nothing

more than a wayward updraft.
        Is it that they fear the lure
           of the spectacle of the plunge

over the cliff to his inevitable
     crash—apotheosis of the thrill-
          seeking harebrained nerd?—that

they want nothing to do
     with the grisly business
          of having to witness a pointless end?

THE TAUBE

First bombs of the war on
Paris Fritz von Hiddeson bombed
café patrons watching
fascinated he dropped
them every night promptly

became known in Paris,
Paris in August 1914
from a Taube
means literally, "dove"

carried two men
who could not look
down every night,
treacherous in wind,
"the six-o'clock Taube"
means literally, café patrons
of history, wing-warper at six, the
German Imperial Air Force
could not look down
unless tilted perilously
                              perilously
treacherous the Taube
fascinated Paris in August 1914
(one of the famous
became known promptly
at six, the first fascinated "dove")
bombed café patrons
were not built after '14
who could look down
at history, fascinated.

How to Save Someone
Who's Hanging from a Cliff
[Stage 3]

In Memoriam Jackson Mac Low 1922–2004

Be careful when grabbing clothes,
for clammy palms ...
With one hand, tell him to
conserve as much energy
near where he is hanging.
Conserve as much energy!
At least one of the victims
stand on a surface.
Have the victim climb as
solid footing. Tell him to
stand on a surface that you are sure *will*
pants (this is no time)—a large boulder, a firm ledge
if you have solid footing. If you are not safe
you may pull him to safety: pull!
Stand on a surface to help you,
solid footing to help you,
hands to clasp, have the victim climb
as if you have solid footing. Tell him to ...
that he needs to hold very still,
that you are sure *will,*
or a live tree. At the bottom of the cliff
if the victim is within reach, a coat, a harness
or a live tree—they
dry your hands—they
try to stay relaxed near where he is hanging
with one hand. Pulling a—
pull him to safety, a large boulder, a firm ledge
if you have solid footing, pulling a
(both end up, that you are sure) *will,*
anything he is wearing, use both:

that he needs to hold very still, as possible.
Panic is not an option. Have the victim climb as
hands to clasp out. If possible, you of adrenaline
pumping through your veins, pulling hands to clasp.
As possible, even his hair will suffice
at the bottom of the cliff.
If you have solid footing, find.

COME TO THE ATTENTION

for simply possession
>> longer
>> and more intense

ILLICITEUPHORIA,EXCITATION,LONG PERIODSOF

>> sleep
>>>> increase includes intent
>>>>> near any person, boats

or other conveyance
>> possess or (to) facilitate
>>> possession a public violates
>>>> regulations which regulate

a variety of
>> aggressive acts
>>> devastating CONSEQUENCES suicides
>>> homicides and

accidents can be
>> denied, will be
>>> addressed with abuse
>>>> s a n c t i o n s

dispensation procedures apply to
>> **all** activities
>>> can be life-threatening all
>>>> must: _cooperate!_

fully expects all to
>> comply with all

work in a fit condition
possible effects

(INCLUDE) possible death

A Concise History of Chaos:
Fremontodendron Californicum and the
Doctrine of Manifest Destiny

Begin with
the scene: set it
up, get a fix on time
if you can: you can't,
you can say it's the end
of winter this bitter March,
all you can say in the face of
countless faces, freeze the data,
lock in to what people call a nasty
March but already Fremontodendron's
pale new growth, fuzzy stems

> *stems initially green, becoming mid-brown in age,*
> *Densely covered with loose, green, becoming*
> *light-brown, Stellate Hairs*

push out from the white brick wall
on which they're espaliered, the shrub's
trunk thick and smooth as a muscular forearm
and, just beginning, shiny yellow flowers—

> *flowers 8 cm wide, single,*
> *Oppositifoliate,*
> *hermaphrodite,*
> *Involucellate,*
> *apetalous,*
> *Pedicellate*

Then begin with John C. Frémont, ex-
senator, ex-governor, ex-major general,
ex-presidential candidate (Republican),
geographer, explorer, cartographer, collector of plants,
surveyor of the west and far west

> *led four expeditions to the far west,*
> *two of them guided by KIT CARSON –*
> *to the Rocky Mountains and to Oregon,*
> *and to Nevada, crossing the SIERRA NEVADA into California.*
> *He discovered FREMONTODENDRON in 'the early 1850s'*
> *the only native member*
> *found in the Sierra Nevada.*

(did he dodge his senatorial duties
one chilly, misty dawn to slip out
and go plant-hunting
on the slopes of the Sierra Nevada?)—
maybe that's why he didn't get re-elected
after just one year in office
but went to Europe

> *where, it is said, he was received by*
> *EMINENT SCIENTISTS AND POLITICIANS*
> *in several countries*

and where undoubtedly he brought with him
the seeds of that prickly plant
Fremontodendron which eventually took hold
in the builders' rubble in the back garden.

I have seen this growing as a tree
in London, England—Wilf

> *Fremontodendron 'CALIFORNIA GLORY'*
> *is a shrub or small tree growing up*
> *to 15 or 20 feet in height, but*
> *as it is SHORT-LIVED may not*
> *reach this size.*

Ours has reached this size.
It is already fifteen to twenty feet in height
and is twelve years old. Its branches,
espaliered on the west-facing wall,
spread the width of the garden
behind our house in London
close by the permanently traffic-clogged
siren-wailed, toxic-fumed air of
the Highbury Corner roundabout.

... it seems to be able to tolerate automobile exhaust.
What a gem!—MaryRuth Casebeer

> *John C. Frémont was called THE PATHFINDER.*
> *He eloped (1841) with JESSIE,*
> *daughter of Senator Thomas Hart Benton,*
> *a champion of the expansionist movement*
> *known as 'MANIFEST DESTINY'.*
> *Benton saw Frémont as a talented explorer*
> *and promoter of the West.*

He found a path to Jessie
he found a path across
the Sierra Nevada to California
he found a path to Europe
he found a path to our garden
where he found himself

in the midst of a campaign
to co-opt the indigenous inhabitants
(he'd already cajoled the Californios
to persuade Washington to annex them):

> *...were it not for his network of Connections*
> *and his knack for political expediency,*
> *he probably would have been a FAILURE many times over.*
> *He had little moral sense*
> *and allowed GREED and AMBITION to rule him.*

he has already knocked off
the ceanothus blue mound, the valerian,
the passion flower and the rhododendron,
and is threatening
the rambling rose, the three varieties of fuchsia,
the two tree peonies, the winter-flowering iris,
the weigela, the Japanese anemone,
the kerria japonica or 'jews mallow',
the clematis Montana, and the hibiscus.
A garden is a display of personality.

> *His personality VERGED at times on the DICTATORIAL.*
> *His critics call him BRAGGART and CHARLATAN –*
> *his supporters point to his COURAGE and his*
> *DETERMINATION to open the West.*

Wizened with winter but promising glory,
John C. Frémont is about to descend yet again
on our pastoral populace,
each branch bandoliered with blooms
which detonate   yellow   yellow   yellow

exploding sun-barbs even on sunless days
peppering London's shades of grey with
the bleached dry light of California,
destabilizing the less aggressive
denizens and promising,
promising brilliant Pacific vistas.

During a four year period in the 1840s,
the national DOMAIN increased
by 1.2 million square miles,
a gain of more than sixty percent. So RAPID
and DRAMATIC was the process of territorial expansion,
that it came to be seen as an INEXORABLE process,
prompting many Americans to insist that their nation
had a 'MANIFEST DESTINY' to dominate.

John C. Frémont bursts into town
as though it were terrain to be opened up
as though we were settlers with Latino names
living in Britain who should be absorbed
into the benevolent states of an America hell-bent
on exerting its great flowering
resources to stun the world with greenbacks.

The ANTHERS are slightly darker and ORANGER
yellow. They are borne on one side
of the upper half of the free filaments.
The anthers are POLYSPORANGIATE,
the sporangia being curled,
and opening by a lengthwise slit.

John C. Frémont is even now setting up his enfilade,
his vanguard on the boundary wall probing
the delicate plants, tender shoots, rehearsing
his ultimate showdown, the wipeout.

Most important of all, perhaps, was the growing sense of
Aɴxɪᴇᴛʏ which Americans felt toward Gʀᴇᴀᴛ Bʀɪᴛᴀɪɴ.
Americans had always been Sᴜsᴘɪᴄɪᴏᴜs of British
activities in the western hemisphere, but inevitably this
Fᴇᴀʀ had grown as the United States began to define
its strategic and economic Iɴᴛᴇʀᴇsᴛs
in terms that extended Bᴇʏᴏɴᴅ its own borders.

Beginning again, every year
we asked Graham to prune and trim,
try to keep some order and control, stem
the arbitrary shove and brash invasion.
but Fremontodendron fought back.

The leathery leaf blades are ovate,
Cᴏʀᴅᴀᴛᴇ at the base, and Pᴀʟᴍᴀᴛᴇʟʏ Vᴇɪɴᴇᴅ and lobed.
The underside is pale green, and Dᴇɴsᴇʟʏ Cᴏᴠᴇʀᴇᴅ
with white and brown Sᴛᴇʟʟᴀᴛᴇ hairs,
known to cause Dᴇʀᴍᴀᴛɪᴛɪs and eye irritation.

He was a prickly man.
He irritated President Lincoln
who relieved him of his command
as Major General of the Western Division
because he arbitrarily decided to free the slaves
before Lincoln was ready to do so
by means of the Emancipation Proclamation.
Frémont also got under the skin

of President James K. Polk
who allowed him to resign his commission
for refusing to obey his superior's orders.

*I have anecdotal reports of respiratory tract IRRITATION
from the hairs covering the foliage
and fruits of FREMONTODENDRON*

When John C. Frémont plucked a hairy leaf
did he suffer from skin irritation, allergic reaction,
or irritation of the respiratory canal?
Doubtless he did not wear protective goggles
as Ashley, who took over from Graham, did.
He also wore a dust mask, long-sleeved shirt,
a hat and gardening gloves, but still
blossomed a skin rash, wept with conjunctivitis,
he gasped and wheezed.

*The mature flower is about 8 cm wide.
It is composed of 5 FUSED SEPALS,
5 STAMENS, arising from a common column,
and a single POINTED STYLE.
The sepals have the same QUINCUNCIAL
ARRANGEMENT as in bud.
They are yellow.*

Fremontodendron California Glory
is also known as California Slippery Elm
and California Flannelbush (drovers
used to fashion horsewhips from it).
It is violently beautiful
and repays your careful husbandry by slyly
biting back, making you writhe and itch.
You wouldn't think of getting rid of it.

WYOMING WHITE-OUT

In the uncertain time
        between certain weathers
                we cannot say for certain

whether morning or after-
        noon—the light
                a certain kind of dark

white—where sky
        ends and land
                begins: we find our

selves in meld,
        empty space where
                nothing appears or

disappears, the ground
        an undecipherable void,
                all history horizontal,

burying beginnings.
        Wait for the lifting
                revealing the shroud.

DISCARDED CLOTHES

So long, elkhide vest
        handstitched for me by
                a half-Sioux guy

met in an atmospheric
        Wyoming bar, you know,
                buffalo head on the wall,

we'd talked to smoky
        music the night through
                after poetry at the school.

Hello to my friend Elke
        who fits it and whose John
                says Okay, it is your style,

it isn't mine since *Time*
        Remembered, jazz and poetry
                East Village gigs.

Goodbye, my fancying
        myself as a with-it dude, bolo
                tie dangling from my neck,

sideburns, black moustache,
        Bill Evans, MJQ, a social toke,
                If you could see me now.

WAITING FOR THE RENDEZVOUS

Glinting in the sun-
      set across the winter river
         the refraction of windows

shivers the view:
      nothing he sees is still,
         not him, not the city, nor the river—

the skyline shimmers
      beyond the windowsill,
         the room where he waits

for her resonates
      in the building
         above the subterranean

rumble of tunnels;
      look away an instant:
         the dark infills interstices

and in the afterglow
      faint lights prick out
         where others prepare

intimate meals, rendezvous
      that animate the stillness above
         the interminable sluicing of the river.

WOODPIGEONS

I spent my whole self searching
love which I thought was you

it was mine so briefly
and I never knew it, or you went

—Frank O' Hara, "Poem"

She arrived with the woodpigeons. That is to say, she arrived
and they left. Not that she had anything obviously to do with
it. Of course she did. She kept on arriving and then she left.
They appeared constantly to be fleeing the roost at her, at his, at
anyone's approach, though clearly they had to have returned in
order to flee again. He never saw them return but they always
fled. She came to stay with him and then she went. They—or
more usually one of them—would explode out of the treetops
with a clatter of wings against foliage that sounded like falling
buckshot, and hurl themselves down to the field below the house,
where they alighted on the rock walls. They waited, longer than
he was prepared to stare at them, or they flew further away. He
had to assume their return, never count on it. By saying hello
to her was he not already beginning to say goodbye? Her eyes
were flecked with green, the same glossy green as on the necks of
woodpigeons. They could be heard from afar cooing in the trees.
They were there, somewhere, part of an elemental landscape
of love and loss. Their departure was sudden, loud, a flight of
hysterical panic. She was of a quiet nature, discreet, but she had
a flighty disposition. Even when he took them for granted, they
all at once insinuated themselves by making a hyper-dramatic
and, he thought, totally uncalled-for statement by ostentatiously
going away and not returning for an indefinite time which was,
for all practical purposes, forever.

MOVING BODIES

The relation between what we are and what we know is never settled. — John Berger, WAYS OF SEEING

I *Point of No Return*

He's been anticipating the moment for the last thousand miles when the last digit on the dial, which shows 99,999, will, by incremental tenths, push all the others into zeros and add one more: a '1'. This is it, he whispers to himself and to the car in which he's lived up and down motorways of déjà vu. At the moment when all the zeros begin lining up evenly, nudging the 1 into its very first appearance on earth, he swings the car into the middle lane to overtake a van that has seen better days, the words E. Veal—Removals stencilled in faded blue on its side. As he is pulling ahead, he looks for a landmark, a feature that he can use in future trips on this stretch of roadway as a reference to mark the achievement of the rite of passage, even a road sign: Diversion, Contraflow, Uneven Surface, the sign for bumps on the road which looks like an ideogram for a woman's breasts, Dead Slow. There is none. On either side are broad, rolling fields. No single tree, no house or outbuilding, no winding country road, no church spire, water tower, pylon, utility pole. Only the curving double band of the motorway punctuated by smaller or larger vehicles in both directions, passing each other or being overtaken. They are all travelling at fractionally different speeds and all are heading toward some temporary ultimate, or ultimately temporary destination.

II *A Free Ride?*

At 104,162 miles his car's mileage indicator has stopped registering, although he has been travelling steadily since that point. For some time he has been proceeding with nothing to show for it, no evidence he has gone anywhere beyond the point at which 104,162 miles was reached. Has he left but never arrived? Is he going nowhere? Is he getting a free ride? Maybe he's repeating journeys he's already made, going over old ground in an endless loop. Maybe he's lying in bed with his eyes closed, still seeing the after-image of the road in dwindling perspective before him. On the other hand, he may have been travelling but the car has not. He cannot be sure that what he takes to be the continuous vibration of the motor is not a steady tone in his ears, the tinnitus of the traveller, the sound of the world whirring. How long, he wonders, would it take him on his own to traverse 104,162 miles? A lifetime? And when he had passed that point, would he be a better man for it? To the left of the motorway some cows are walking slowly from one side of a field to the other, their heads close to the ground.

III *An Event*

It is clear that he and the car parted company at a specific point in time occasioned by an event that occurred at 104,162 miles— which establishes the distance covered up until the event but not the time nor the event itself. On long journeys time expands to fill the space created by tedium, as the numbers on the dial creep inexorably up, the first impinging on the second, the second on the third, and so on, as thoughts provoke further thoughts. A car is a personal, private space. Being inside one resembles the feeling of being inside a room in which the windows are made of one-way glass, looking from the inside out. Here intimate acts are performed in the illusion that one has total privacy: noses are picked, crotches scratched, food eaten with no manners while listening to loud music. People kiss and fondle each other, and engage in sexual acts on the back seat. Or the front seat. An event of just such a private nature, or an accumulation of such events which reached a critical mass, must have made it impossible for him and the car to proceed further together. The car went one way and he another. One-way systems are notorious for separating people from their objectives. The possibility of knowing what the event, or events, might have been depends on the ability to recall what happened a few thousand miles ago, which is fruitless since corners have been turned, a multitude of events has transpired since then, and the car has made up its own mind and it would be futile to argue. You don't argue with a machine.

IV *A Hypothesis*

The car stops recording miles in the way a brain stops recording memories, as after a traumatic episode, a disconnect affecting the motor neuron axons. Moving parts may suffer metal fatigue, wires corrode, power fail. A collision with a dragon can occur at three o'clock in the morning. My God, a dragon, he shouts and slams on the brakes, swerving the car on to the hard shoulder. The creature, the size of a very large dog, stares into the headlamps. Its eyes are red. Its open mouth displays rows of long, needle-like teeth and a forked tongue, like a lizard's. Its head is somewhat the shape of a Doberman's only longer, and scaly. Its wings hang from its shoulders like two limp fans. No fire issues from its nostrils, which are flared. The beast slowly raises itself on its kangaroo-like hind legs, its long curled tail writhing, and rather clumsily crosses the verge into the surrounding darkness.

V *The Phantom Access Road*

Isn't the essence of travel movement, change? He still feels the same, but that something has changed is evident when he travels north again over the same spaghetti junction. The first time, going slowly because of heavy traffic, his road crosses over a gently curving slip road, also held aloft by stanchions, which carries traffic diagonally below him and to the right over a third road, which is on the ground. The second time, a few days later, he crosses at exactly the same place and again is forced to slow down. There is no road in the air beneath him. A third and fourth time the same slowing down for no perceptible reason, the same absence of the slip road. It has either disappeared or it didn't exist in the first place. He knows it exists because he saw it. He has faith in his original vision even though he has not seen that road to this day. He has come to see the void as confirmation that everyone may have seen better days. The past is before him. He and animals move about, everything else ought to stay where it belongs virtually forever, relatively. Continuity, if not sanity, depends on art not reality.

VI *The Butterfly Effect*

Stuck in a tailback, he sees the same family of four in the car next to him at different stages of sensitive dependence on initial conditions. What these conditions are may be determined by people, or animals, ahead of him, perhaps so far ahead they can never be traced, much less caught up with and brought to account. The children in the back seat register either annoyance or jubilation whenever they fall behind or overtake him. Which is the fastest queue in front of the toll booth, petrol pumps, airport check-in desks? Can life prepare him to put into practice Large Deviations Theory to contend with queues? They pull ahead, and then he does. They pull into his lane in front of him but in a few moments the lane they were in surges ahead. They manage to cross back over, draw level and pass him. The boy in the back seat smirks. Then he catches up and passes them. The boy averts his gaze. And so it goes for several miles until the effect wears itself out. Hands clap, a dog barks, church bells peal. Something happened because somebody somewhere did something at some time that caused something else to happen, perhaps on the other side of the globe.

PASSAGE

A ship moves close
to the shore in the night, running

lights catch the waves in,
the waves are drawing the shore

closer to the ship, everybody is
moving closer, nobody

sees they are moving
bodies on the water at night, drawing

closer to the moving ship, already
my body has moved with the waves' reaching

in to the white shore, the ship rides the
swells in so I'm reaching it, near

enough so I hear the thump of
its engine through my bones, so

it courses through the body I have
left standing on the beach

LONDON BUDDLEIA

Drops in where it's not wanted
    in waste ground and town garden,
        cracks in the brickwork,

snakes up downspouts,
    prises fingerlings
        through basement gratings,

sprays purple sprigs from chimneys,
    hangs out on worn steps
        huddles, dusty in doorways

and at the base of railings, slumps
    under the railway bridge, straggling
        its supplicating tendrils.

Finding what nourishment it may
    even in times of drought,
        it has a rickety lushness, the old soak,

that I pretend studiously to ignore:
    not the soft touch of butterflies
        who give their tithe in kind.

DREAM CITY

It is always never there except
when I'm there, I'm always
there when people look at me
as they pass me on the street
telling me of their adventures
across the river, urging me
to accompany them, but I'm not
there, I'm in another part of the city
where I'm looking at people
who remind me of people
I used to know and who aren't
there any more, they could be
in another part of the city
looking for me.

Dust

The city's blowing away
in a leaden wind of hydrocarbons,
pizza crumbs, droppings, seeds,
dust and desiccated leaves, fæces
and pieces of paper heaped
in gutters and pavement cracks,
clogging drains and my nose,
gritting my eyes, furring my mouth
so I end up ingesting it in spite
of myself——city distillate,
embodiment of multitudes——
one day to discover my dust
drifting in seams of the city.

THE APPROACH

Slipping under cloud cover
on the glide path we're tipped
into the city from the edge,
skimming terraces and playing fields,
a sudden touch down, hurled
forward with reverse thrust
so our bodies re-live the familiar
connection so narrowly made.

I've got wheels not wings: the way
to get there is cycle, car, train,
tube, the No. 19 Routemaster
trusty as old legs though prone
to the usual decrepitude, over
soil, steel, the made-up bumps,
hills, valleys, straightaways of our solid
city on the level, and not nothingness
making my palms sweat despite
the jets' whine and grumbling
which one day must flame out, reiterating
how fleeting the world, so easily lost.

Oh, sure, from my windowseat at night
London's a spiderweb string of raindrops
glimmering in the wind:
I'm mired in the mud, but then,
there's water, that other part of me
I'm closer to at sea level
where I need not fall to be.

Half Life

Half life was lived in the deep
sepia underground getting
there, wherever, Piccadilly,
Paris, under the city, river,
whatever, sliding and climbing
through Piranesi's gigantic night-
time purgatories in an infolding
of passages, steps, subways
and underpasses, waiting on
the station platform where walls
are tiled like a morgue.

And half is spent listening
to the strangely reassuring beat
of trains pounding the track
under our sound box of a house
built over a web of tunnels
(the circulation of the city!)
pulsing in the nether world
which mimics my own, where
the escalator winds me down.

STAIRS

Conduct you to another place
a passage on the way that tilts
you into a different, more certain state.

At the top of the stairs feeling light-
headed, nearer the small deaths
of sleeping and dreaming, the skylight
lets in a square of the firmament;
the roof terrace and parapet
beckon you to the splendid view:
the solitary roofer straddles the ridge.

Descending may be quicker,
legs dance down tunnels,
crowds swept underground
and streamed into the perpetual
interchange, bearing their urgencies,
the everyday but necessary messages.

But always that part of yourself left
on the stairs, as you step from
a higher or lower plane,
the old not yet done,
the new not yet begun.

THE REPEAT

I thought suppose the escalator cut out
just like that, the ground out from under
everybody's body going up, coming down,
and going down, going down further, farthest
so all tangled, crushed: but all continued after
all emptying out just as before, before

I was thinking of running, getting
the hell out but breathing
suddenly heavily difficult, became
impossible, in fact, clouds clogged
all breath, wreathed. I broke out
just, in time, in a sweat
my legs striding me away
and up steadily, arms bearing
wing-like, streets roofs below
slipping out of sight, in this blue,
this really brilliant space, incredibly
uncrowded where it seemed
I could, you know, just go.

I ask myself why do I repeat all this
night after night, running
and falling and rising again, and again,
as I repeat the words of love to you
when we doubt not breathing?

SONG OF THE CITIES
After 9/11/01

Walt bequeathed himself to the dirt
but small pieces of me are already layered
in dusty London, dead cells have flaked
and danced in the traffic's breeze, and my hair,
snipped in drifts on the hairdresser's floor,
doubtless reposes at this very moment
in a landfill site north of the North Circular Road.

When a boy, blood from my eyebrow poured
down my nose and into the Edgware mud
where I'd slipped as my fingers missed their grip
on a fencepost, and my sweat has rained
onto the pavement as I ran from a loutish gang;
I left a half-pound of flesh, "uniform adipose tissue,
a benign lipoma," ten years ago in a bin
in St. Bartholomew's Hospital from where
it was probably incinerated
and dispersed in the city air we breathe.

My foothold is tenon'd and mortis'd in granite,
and I know what he meant because my invisible
footsteps are impressed forever in New York's
conglomerate and in the tar of its streets
covered and preserved by new tar.
At times late at night returning from some convivial
drinking or even not so convivial drinking,
I have pee'd in the street when caught short
and New York streets were golden with me.

I have helped to wear down the steps to Riverside
Park, thin the already thinning grass of Prospect Park,
I've pruned and cut and planted in the Brooklyn backyard,

the soil has jammed itself under my fingernails and dusted
under my collar. I compose the city where the dust
of thousands is carted off to vast landfills
which shall rise in hills and form the new city.

What is the city but a composition of millions
who have lived and died there? The fallen will be
compacted into the foundations of tall buildings,
and underneath, the subways will thump and vibrate,
a living heart. The city rises in impersonal
commemoration, and we inhabit the idea
resurrected again each time a building falls.

THE CONVERGENCE
for Maggie

1

The ways converge
as montage, our lives

overlaid upon a grid
of streets directing us

toward our inter-
section: we fall into step.

We circumscribe
ourselves the way

we become familiar
with neighbourhoods.

We speak whole streets—
flaneurs of avenues,

accidence of friends newly
connected—encounter

ourselves in intimate
stories, make straight

a path, negotiate the con-
junctions, changes of address

on the way: step out.

2

Every day I see jets home in
to this city, trails tracked

on controllers' screens, montage
of many connections over

a virtual city. The real city arises
at first from a confusion

of dereliction and scaffolding
and becomes slowly known by

the recapitulation of each
vertical, each cross-member

on the city plan mimicking
a building whose armature

of girders supports
the shape of things to be

revealed within the structure
of neighbourhoods, the life

of streets leading to possibilities.

3

A lone aviator once circled
the old city in an invisible

holding pattern
he could not guess at,

as you and I also remained
unaware of the concentric,

the ever-narrowing circles
drawing us in for a soft landing.

AT THE CONTROLS

manning the controls, faith
is required, instruments
must perform, the slightest
nudge on the joystick
to keep on course
for the rush at touchdown

figures from the past
flicker in front of me,
hands waving hello
or goodbye? the re-run
I'm always playing
without clothes on
friends around me
lurching as we
hurtle down the open
tarmac, hangups forgotten

let us ride the airwaves
open up conversations
beyond the cockpit
seize the hands
that reach out to us,
forget the fallibility
of engines bearing us up
that could let us down
why not believe that forward
movement will keep us
buoyant: a will, a kind of act

ELEGY FOR THE FALLING MAN

I

kicking down the gates to break
free, he lights out for the territory
unafraid to touch the wild-
life, in the peaceable kingdom
where coyote circles to sniff
the sleeping traveller's head,
footprints in the morning loping
away toward the distant range,
rattler in the ditch reminding him
two's a crowd in a narrow space

II

falling to the ground he strikes
out for the territory of metal,
the pump-action weapon he uses
to clear the tree of red-breast trash—
in his trigger-finger he discovers
he's God who takes away, his fury
at the hopping multitude
on the blood-spattered ground,
counting on no comeback, no song

CRACKING THE AIR-SHELL

Cracking the air-shell he staggers out wholly
unprepared, the trace-memory of being
comfortably enveloped breaking up like
a dicey mobile phone connection—
Can I get back to you? but his answer's lost
in the white noise of outer space, infinite
tailbacks, wrecks in the middle of the carriageway,
a jack-knifed lorry sliming its load
over the roadway. Chassis crumples softly
into chassis. *Where are you?* he hears
before the line crashes again. He wishes
he was cocooned again with the radio playing
L'enfant et les sortilèges, the traffic flowing
normally up and down, everyone speaking
the air controllers' language, planes
staying up, nothing down, the
sealed system humming with blood.

LEAR IN MANHATTAN
After 9/11

Stumbling when he saw, what
did he see?—the futility
of lives tethered to the 9-to-5
in the money-palaces
greed inflated to crazy heights—

or a miracle reprieve down here
in the murk and debris, drifts
of bills and memos to you and me,
dust he could not help but breathe
in the terrible stink of mortality?

AFTER 'THE FLIGHT FROM SMOKY EDGE'

What was that mise-en-scène again—
    floaters, spotted figures flashing
        before his eyes—

desperate on awakening to fix
    the after-image of flying, or gliding:
        it's fragmenting, but the residue of

elation's left, that confident, casual pleasure
    of being in one's element, when
        letting go his child-grip on the swing

at apogee, he flew a quarter-orbit
    before a rolling landing on the grass
        further by a foot than his fellows.

The uncaged birds are doing a flit and he's
    trying to reconstruct his lines
        leveraged from a fade-out

scene in which he plays the lead
    in the early-morning show,
        self's interlocutor.

Come back! Speak up! But the players,
    front-lit, lose the plot behind the scrim,
        exeunt in slow dissolve.

MUSIC FOR THE RETREAT

US Air Force Base at RAF Lakenheath

At first the sound—like surf, like spiccato strings—could be
mistaken for a far-off aircraft approaching, but then defines
itself as the taped drum roll over the Tannoy, prelude
to *God Save the Queen* and *The Star Spangled Banner*, the signal
for all to halt, stand at attention, stop all cars, salute (if in
       uniform),
everyone stuck where they are, waiting for the honour guard to
lower the flags at end of day, shifting from foot to foot while the
scratchy anthems grind on as if played on a decrepit wax cylinder
squawkbox at Ladysmith or San Juan Hill, but this is F-111
country, at intervals around the clock they roar off the runway
crushing all thought and sense of things proportionate,
       scattering the birds.

           The solo clarinet in *Abîme des oiseaux*,
the third movement of Messiaen's *Quatuor pour la fin du temps*,
describes in dark, slow tempo a welling up of night-time
sleepless moans, the collective despair of those trapped
in arbitrary incarceration, endless time, as Messiaen
and five thousand others were in Stalag VIII A.

        At the first performance, January 15, 1941,

The cold was excruciating, the Stalag buried under snow.
The four performers played on broken-down instruments...
the cello had only three strings, the keys of my piano went down
but did not come up again. Our costumes were unbelievable:
they rigged me out in a green jacket completely in shreds,
and I wore wooden clogs...

In the middle section the clarinet soars into birdsong
rising beyond boundaries to pierce the perimeter fence:

Never has my music been listened to with more attention and understanding than on that occasion.

On the base the grammar of is becomes the rhetoric of must punctuated by the raucous drum-roll, the raptor's scream banishing songbirds, the music always the sound of power.

THE LEAP

Let's essay some kind of miracle
          hovering   arms outstretched in free
               fall as though skydiving except

there's no parachute only
          arteries and veins   twigs and branches
               and the song of birds to sustain you.

Why not, in other words, just let go
          trust in the tree gently to net you
               to earth, and once there you may

look up and gauge the amazing
          space you've tumbled through
               to get to where you dreamed to be.

         *

Here he is being watched
          by birds sitting in a tree
               while he whizzes by

trying, or not, to fly.
          They think he will likely die,
               maybe not if the tree

comes between him and a hard
          landing. Thing about landing—
               how well they know!—

is to have feathers
       to soften the blow.
              He doesn't, of course, as anyone

can see, those colourful birds
       that light up the tree
              as he flashes by on some crazy dream.

*

In the treetops living got to be
       a bore, but he had to try
              to justify his *idée fixe*

that we have this compelling
       trace memory
              of the monkey life, swinging

from branch to branch—or that
       we feel more secure
              with our two feet up in the air

instead of planted on terra firma
       along with every other
              murderous creature—or was it

simply to witness and shame rapacious
       developers raping the countryside?
              So: the big leap forward

into the firmament (falling
       is the quickest way to go)
              knowing he will be upheld.

After 'The Island (with constant chaos)'

For Art & Science cannot exist but in minutely
organised particulars.
        —William Blake

Flora in their motley pots array
    insouciant faces with sang-froid.

When she's not looking they creep
    closer and closer and sooner

rather than later completely
    infiltrate the remaining space

with their pinks and yellows and blues,
    intimidate her with showy beauty

their urge to deflower
    and propensity to fade into

decrepitude, enfold her
    memory mulching into entropy.

        *

My life she thinks is measured out
    in colourful pottery collected

in country village studio shops.
    'Dropping in' she's fired

by the hunt, asks to see the kiln,
    then retreats from that violent heat

spying the one-and-only
        on sagging shelves.

One has bred dozens, allotropic
        scenes, the torrid and the horrible,

painted glaze of moments
        savoured and as quickly lost.

            *

How the bric-a-brac and
        bricolage clutter the concept.

Sometimes the sofa's the only place
        to think of sex and furniture,

how randomised particulars press in
        and violate that private space.

She feels like hurling the crockery
        and pots across the room

but might hit the cat.
        Make straight a path

through the wilderness
        where one geegaw begets another.

Let me re-arrange the mugs and vases
        Spirit of the Dead Watching.

Come and get me, she whispers, before
        I perish of the gimcrack world.

Connection—Collection

You could say there's a connection between
two people fucking, you can say that again,

and again she sits on his lap
on just the right kind of chair

the kind with padded arms for her legs
to rest on without welting

so she can lower herself on
him just so far so

there's a little space between
to, you know, move up

and down. It's one way to make
the connection and has the advantage

of novelty if you haven't tried it
a frisson amongst the breakables

cluttering the table, floor, chairs,
everywhere, that define him:

hold on a moment, you mean
what you accumulate tells

who you are? she knows
he's a natural accumulator

just about every day or every
other day. That says something

about him but not everything, no,
there's more to him than a collection

of spermatozoa, he feels, he has
a sense of beauty, he does, truth

and the rest of it, perceptiveness,
revealing itself for instance in ceramics,

the husbanding of mugs and cups
to kiss and quaff from, he's a quaffer.

He likes the helter-skelter which could be
confused with chaos or at least

disorganisation but isn't because
he knows, he just does,

that disorder in all things
is divine, an orderly disorder,

speed up, he says, as she
goes faster and faster and the order
begins to fracture and heave.

                    *

She's tired of it, she has to remove herself
from this place, him:

I can't stand this retrograde
feng shui, I need a different habitat

where everything is built
around life-support by people

who have an idea where everything
belongs, know its function and purpose.

He considers the proposition:
everything can be re-arranged.

Deckchairs on the Titanic, she sneers,
people don't have to live like this.

A sense of order is relative, he says,
the two of us, our bodies' order and propinquity.

You can have your fucking propinquity,
she ejaculates, I'm going to scream.

How an Airplane Stays Up

Take two kitchen chairs facing each other.
Place a plank extending from one to the other.
Climb on to the plank.
The downward force—you—should equal
the upward force exerted by chairs and plank.

This little demo tells you
all you need to know about the terror
and uncertainty of flying
and nothing about being secure.
The plank might crack and you
crash to the floor, the chairs might
tip, and you along with them,
a sudden wrong move and off you go,
an earthquake could topple
the whole shebang.

This demo is not about airplanes
but fear and chance and fate
the vicissitudes and miseries
of modern life.
The only thing you can count on
between you and disaster
is a thin plank.
You better believe it.

Sausage Thief

You might think I'm chasing a dog
who's nipped a string off my chipolata link
and is running off with it
frisking insolently just out of reach. No.

The fact is we're engaged in a circus act duet
where I'm the angry, ineffectual clown
and she the highly trained terrier wafting
the filched meat before my nose. No.

The fact is we're having a doggy game
where she darts and dances and I prance
down the street shouting and brandishing
a pair of outsize shears as if to cut off her tail. No.

The fact is the dog is my displaced lover
who has bobbitted my penis by leaving me
and I'm acting out my sublimated feelings
by going for her with murderous intent. No.

The fact is I'm leading too tranquil a life
and nurture an unfulfilled wish
to engage in violent and shocking acts
which provide an outlet for repressed hostility. No.

The fact is I love dogs and wish them no harm.
When asked a 'security question' on what pet
I'd most like to have, I always choose a dog
even though that bitch stole my sausage.

Hoeing

Hidden by lap fencing you
      have to jump up to see
            over, an urban lost domain

of allotments clings to
      the side of the railway cutting:
            the scene of archaic rites

of planting, weeding, harvesting
      by two women recapitulating
            with their hoes the back-bending

movement of Millet's gleaners
      scavenging in the stubble for
            broken pieces of cabbage leaves

or the undug tiny potato.
      But this cyclic repetition
            of a timeless choreography is

no less formal an enterprise, fulfils
      no greater need: who's to gainsay
            these two in floral smocks adorned

who dance the dance they themselves
      initiate to honour Ceres and by the bye
            add garden-variety to the ordinary?

FLYER

Clearly the Dawn of the Age of Flight
is already fading into jerky Movietone snow:

the medium makes the process
of throwing yourself into the firmament

fundamentally a bash,
the biplane's doped linen skin

a fleshly substance you could poke
a hole in a cloud through.

But the black-robed bearded patriarch standing
on a stepladder, one hand resting on the fuselage—

a benediction? a balancing act?—is solid.
God meant man to fly,

his uprightness testifies, and who are we
to gainsay him? We do it all the time

in our streetclothes for purposes
not necessarily connected with religion.

We spy in the sky.
Who knows who looks down on you?

This is a blessing, as our fathers knew
who gaped on the grass
at the first Immelmann turn.

FERRY

Which is moving, the quayside
        or the ferry as it slips
                into night taking him

to the other side, another island
        dimly seen, the familiar outlines
                of where he's been with her

always in his mind, senses awakened
        by obscure scents eddying
                between drift and direction

lassitude and necessity always
        aboard or ashore, the nearer
                to one the further from the other

                        but never far from either.

                *

What is moving is his heart
        his head in that other place
                over the water, demarcation

between the solitary and conjoined,
        view of misty shapes of the unreal
                city arising at water's edge

slowly approaching *vita nuova*
        city of shameless desires
                anticipated and enacted

for a time, and then the return
across the water to that other
world of works and days.

BIRD MAN

Look, I swear there are no wires.
I don't have a rocket motor strapped to my back.
No tricks with lights, it's outdoors isn't it.

Sure, you need a kind of strength,
and I don't mean just to flap the wings: stamina
to withstand the buffeting of the wind,

a certain dexterity to warp the wings.
You slip in the slipstreams of passing craft,
you're prey to extremely large raptors, the roc

and some you haven't heard of.
Although it all depends on you
it helps to have a partner.

Why do I do it? It's quiet up here,
drifting and skimming over the crazy-quilt
mother ground: I like the rush.

OK, you want advice? Here's advice.
Don't get too high, the Icarus effect and all that.
Buoyancy can fail, you may
fall: don't give a damn. Behave like a butterfly.
Develop a head for heights.
Nobody said it was easy.
Landing's a downer.

After 'Hutch'

And here's a picture of me
        on the hillside overlooking the sea
                with you, my daughter, you're not

concerned the animals are not
        in the hutch, they seem not
                concerned, they're lying down

in the grass in front of
        the hutch overlooking
                the sea, having had

one assumes, enough of munching
        we're not holding hands
                I have my back to you, looking

out to sea, you must be
        there because I sense you
                there, the animals are out

enjoying their lie-down and not
        in their hutch which is where,
                one assumes, they rest, or sleep

you're very small, my daughter,
        a baby, really, even though you're not,
                you're holding your doll but not

my hand, I cannot see your face
        or mine in the picture, so
                cannot tell what we might be

thinking, perhaps we're thinking
      that the animals seem unconcerned
            by you and me standing

in their hillside field by the sea
      or that this is how, though differing
            in size and years, not even able to see

each other, ever, and forever
      in this picture, we are close
            to one another, though not

acknowledging each other's
      presence, so unconcerned, though
            there you are forever at my back.

OUTSIDE YOUR KITCHEN WINDOW
N R V D 1904–2004

Either life begins outside
your kitchen window, or
the world ends, the western world
at least, off Cape Clear and the Fastnet:
the mood, or the day, or the weather
depending.

This morning outside your kitchen window
all proceeds at its normally murderous
pace, magpies and crows rematerialising
themselves from out there somewhere
dive-bombing each other
off the birdfeeder leaving
the politely taupe collared doves
to leverage crumbs and leftovers
shaken from the tablecloth.

A peaceable kingdom of sorts
or a pecking order, even the cat
slinking under the bushes dreaming
he's wilder than he is and not
coddled and cuddled and overfed.
No-one ever goes hungry in your house.

My life can end now, you said
outside your kitchen window
where tables and chairs were set up
for your hundredth, and you holding court
in the sun and everyone
nicked bits of the scene
with their digitals, and the Rector
read out the formal letter from the President.

The sou'wester gets up
outside your kitchen window,
the teenagers in lifejackets huddle
in their scudding Lasers tacking
in the force 3 on the bay, and the windsurfers
cream downwind, wakes criss-crossing
the Josephine's with her boatload
of early returning shoppers
and Sherkin day-trippers
debarking at Abbey Strand.

Gulls and terns stream past
your kitchen window: the Atlantic front looms
and blackens the sky, the shore below invisible.
Rain lashes the house; for days after
Irish mist shrouds the trees with droplets

outside your kitchen window: the cannon
by the lifeboat house booms over the bay
summoning the crew to head out to sea.
When the weather breaks
a thin wedge of orange-red lacquers
the blackness over Mount Gabriel

outside your kitchen window: six celebrants
plough their wake across the bay in a Zodiac:
the Rector, your son and daughter-in-law,
grandson, boat owner and his six-year-old son.
Your son steadies you, or what is left
in an urn between his knees
let not your heart be troubled
and we set our course for the trackless

sea-path outside your kitchen window:
Whither I go ye know, and the way ye know

off Horseshoe Harbour on Sherkin Island
where, Ruardhi knows, the sea
is calmer. He cuts the engine, we drift
on the swell, *let not your heart be troubled,*
neither let it be afraid, intones Bruce,
signalling your son who removes the lid:
we here commit the ashes of our sister Nini
to the sea, earth to earth, ashes to ashes…

outside your kitchen window:
I go to prepare a place for you
as the birds of the air, and he
shall change our mortal body.

Notes

A number of these poems were written using works of art as a point of departure. Where the title of the work is not evident in the poem, they are listed as they appear in the book as follows: 'My Order Is Not Your Order', after Bryan Ingham, *Head (dark version)*, 1996, etching; 'The Meeting', after the paintings of Jeremy Annear; '*Nature Morte*', after Vanessa Gardiner, *Boscastle* series, 2001–2002, acrylic on plyboard; 'Conjugal Love Poem', after Howard Hodgkin, *Realism*, 2001, oil on wood; 'The Language of Animals', after Paula Rego, *Encampment*, 1989, etching and aquatint; 'Do Angels Eat?' after Albrecht Dürer, *Melencolia I*, 1514, engraving; 'Discarded Clothes', after Howard Hodgkin's painting of the same title, 1985–90, oil on wood; 'After "The Flight from Smoky Edge"', after Stephen Chambers's etching of the same title, 2005.

Poems from *The Guts of Shadows* were written to accompany images by John Wright, as follows: 'Dream City', *Dream City,* 2002, oil and mixed media; 'The Approach', *Raft of the Medusa*, 2002, oil, mixed media and collage; 'Half Life', 'Stairs' and 'The Repeat', *Study for 'Stairs',* mixed media and collage, 2003; 'Song of the Cities', *Song of the Cities*, 2003; 'Music for the Retreat', *Music for the Retreat*, 2003, oil and mixed media; 'The Convergence', *An Affair of Cities*, 2003, oil and mixed media; 'At the Controls', *Vol de nuit*, 2002, oil, mixed media and collage; 'Elegy for the Falling Man', *The Falling Man*, 2003, acrylic and mixed media; 'Cracking the Air-Shell', *History of Time*, 2003, oil and mixed media; 'Lear in Manhattan', *Lear in Manhattan*, 2002, oil and mixed media.

Poems from *Leaping Down to Earth* were written after images by Stephen Chambers and Tom Hammick, as follows: after Stephen Chambers: 'The Leap', *The Leap (with Turkish finches)*, 2006, oil; 'After "The Island (with constant chaos)"', *The Island (with constant chaos),* 2006, oil; 'Connection-Collection', *Connection-Collection*, 2003, oil; 'How an Airplane Stays Up', *The Demonstrator*, 2003, etching with chine collé; 'Sausage Thief', *The Sausage Thief of St Avit (nocturnal)*, 2008, screenprint with inkjet and intaglio. After Tom Hammick: 'Hoeing', *Harvest*, 2007, etching, aquatint, and spitbite; 'Flyer', *Flyer III*, 2004, etching and aquatint; 'Ferry', *Ferry*, 2008, edition variable soft ground etching; 'Bird Man', *Birdmen*, 2004, drypoint; 'After "Hutch"', *Hutch*, 2005, edition variable etching; 'Outside Your Kitchen Window', *Kitchen Window*, 2004, oil on linen.

Speak To Me Silently: Still Life and Poetry
Stay me with flagons: Song of Solomon 2:5
If you're depicting something made ... Patrick Caulfield, 1936–2005, as
quoted in Marco Livingstone, *Patrick Caulfield: Paintings*. Aldershot,
Lund Humphreys, 2005, p.75. The poem is after Caulfield's 'Café
Interior: Afternoon,' 1973, oil on canvas, private collection.
Joanna ... Michael: Joanna and Michael Mosse Pottery, founded 1980,
specialised in slip and sgraffito decorated salt glazed stoneware.
Taylor-Wood: Sam Taylor-Wood, b.1967 London. British film, video
and conceptual artist.
Meléndez: Luis Meléndez, 1715–1780. 'Still Life with Pomegranates,
Apples, Azaroles, and Grapes in a Landscape', 1771, oil on canvas, The
Prado, Madrid. Meléndez is considered the greatest still-life painter
of 18th-century Spain and one of the finest European painters of the
genre.
The four seasons ... : adapted from the royal commission to Meléndez
from Prince Charles III, later King Charles IV, and his wife, Princess
Maria Luisa.
Julia: The British painter and printmaker Julia Farrer, b.1950.
[1] Natura Morta: Giorgio Morandi, 1890–1964. 'Natura morta,' 1941,
oil on canvas, lot 58 in Christie's Italian Sale, 16 October 2009.
[2] The in and the out of it: Morandi, 'Natura morta con cinque oggetti,'
1956, etching, Vitali 116, Calcografia Nazionale, Rome.

'The Lascaux Variations: Fractals of Being'
Since 1963 the caves at Lascaux have been closed to the public
in an effort to prevent the deterioration of the images caused by
carbon dioxide exhaled by crowds of visitors. The visitor now sees
an exact underground reconstruction of the caves including faithful
reproductions of the paintings.

Colour-beginning: In his watercolours of the second decade of the
19th century, J.M.W. Turner "would begin a composition over the
barest sketch, in colour alone, blocking in the principal masses and
tones, establishing the overall structure of the design in colour, not
in line. Sometimes this would serve as underpainting for the finished
watercolour; sometimes, however, ... the 'colour-beginning' is a
separate exercise, exploratory, as it were, rather than preparatory.
Later, indeed, it became an activity on its own ..." Andrew Wilton,
"Turner's Drawings and Watercolours," *Turner 1775–1851*, catalogue
of the exhibition of 16 November 1974–2 March 1975, London, Tate

Gallery, 1974, p.26. A number of these "colour-beginnings" can be found in the Tate's Turner Bequest.

The quotation in italics is from Georgio Morandi—see note to *Preface*.

'Conjugal Love Poem'

I started this poem by turning the platitude "Nothing is as it seems" on its head, because I felt Hodgkin was being playfully ironical by calling his painting "Realism". What is real, he appears to be saying, is what I think (or paint) it as being. I call this poem "Conjugal Love Poem" because two people in a long-lasting close relationship may accept diversity as contributing to rather than detracting from their affinity. The traditional regularity of the form, a villanelle, does not accord with what the poem is saying, another instance of the paradox I see in the painting.

'Edgar Allan Poe Awakens in Islington'

'For the Love of God, / Montresor!' *The Cask of Amontillado.*

'A Backward Glance at the Past of the Futuristic Present'.

'Rayist'. A theory first propounded by Mikhail Larionov in the book *Rayism*, 1913, with images by himself and Nataliya Goncharova. Susan P. Compton writes: "In it he set out his new theory under the Russian title *Luchizm*, which has usually been translated as 'rayonnism'. Although this is a correct French translation of *luchizm*, an exact English equivalent is ray-ism. Presumably because the style was first noticed in western Europe in the French press, the word *rayonnisme* was simply taken over by the English-speaking historians who did not realise the meaning of the Russian original." *The World Backwards: Russian Futurist Books 1912–16* (London, The British Library, 1978), p.32. Larionov explained the theory thus: "We do not sense the object with our eye, as it is depicted conventionally in pictures and as a result of following this or that device; in fact we do not sense the object as such. We perceive a sum of rays proceeding from a source of light: these are reflected from the object and enter our field of vision … Rayism is concerned with spatial forms that can arise from the intersection of the reflected rays of different objects, forms chosen by the artist's will." p.89.

'Forms of Movement'

Forms of Movement (Galliard) is the title of a copper sculpture, 1965, by Barbara Hepworth, in the Tate St. Ives. The quotations in italics are from the writings of Barbara Hepworth.

'Normandy Beaches 2008'

The poem is a conflation of events and observations I made mainly at Utah Beach and also at Omaha Beach, together with verbatim accounts by members of the Allied Invasion Force (Operation Overlord) of the landings on D-Day, 6 June 1944, and reactions to the landings by members of the German forces. The accounts are acknowledged in the following source notes. For general information and maps I consulted Stephen Badsey, *Battle Zone Normandy: Utah Beach*, Sutton Publishing, Stroud, 2004, and *Utah Beach to Cherbourg (6 June–27 June 1944)*, CMH Pub.100–12, Washington, D.C., Center of Military History, United States Army, 1990, internet edition at www.history.army.mil/BOOKS/WWII/utah/utah.htm. My thanks to Elke de Wit and John Gorick for their hospitality in Normandy and for making it possible for me to visit the relevant sites.

OTL. Friedrich-August von der Heydte
    Fighting the Invasion: The German Army at D-Day, David C. Isby, ed. London, Greenhill, 2000, pp.227–228.
Pfc. Monico C. Amador
    www.normandy1944.info/veterans/monico_amador.htm
A.C. Lamey   www.ddaymuseum.co.uk/memory_naval.htm
Franz Gockel
    www.bbc.co.uk/history/worldwars/wwtwo/dday_gockel2.shtml
Reg A. Clarke
    www.bbc.co.uk/ww2peopleswar/stories/98/a1144298.shtml
Lieut. Cmdr. A.W. Chappell
    www.bbc.co.uk/ww2peopleswar/stories/96/a5351096.shtml
Brig. Gen. Theodore Roosevelt, Jr. A famous line, recounted in many sources.
Sgt. Thomas Valence
    www.pbs.org/wgbh/amex/dday/sfeature/sf_voices_04.html
Capt. John C. Ausland
    www.normandy1944.info/veterans/john_ausland.html

'The Taube'

Treated text based on William E. Barrett, *The First War Planes*, Greenwich, CT, Fawcett, 1960.

'How to Save Someone Who's Hanging from a Cliff'
Text from David and Joe Borgenicht, *The Action Hero's Handbook*,
London, 2002, selection reprinted in the *Daily Telegraph*, 26 Dec.,
2002, and subjected to chance procedure dictated by the spinning of
a roulette wheel ("0" = free choice) in three stages. In Stage 1, each
line was numbered sequentially and ordered according to the number
that came up. Length of lines was governed by width of the newspaper
column. In Stage 2, the treated version's lines were divided into two at
naturally occurring points, i.e., syntactical units, cæsuras, etc., each of
the two halves having the same number; the roulette wheel was then
spun twice, once for the first half and once for the second, resulting in
two different halves (or not, as chance would have it) combined into
a new line. In Stage 3, punctuation was introduced, a few anomalies
were ironed out, and some lines were re-divided. No words were added.

'Come to the Attention'
Re-working of text from a US Air Force guide for military members
on 'substance abuse.'

'A Concise History of Chaos'
The material in the information boxes is taken from Stewart Robert
Hinsley, "Fremontodendron californicum", The Malvaceae Info website
www.malvaceae.info, "Fremontodendron Gallery" and "The
Fremontodendron Pages", © 2002, 2004 Stewart R. Hinsley;
MaryRuth Casebeer, "The Flannelbush", from *Sierra Foothills Chapter
Newsletter*, reprinted in *The Bay Leaf*, publication of The California
Native Plant Society East Bay Chapter (Alameda & Contra Costa
Counties), Berkeley, California, April 2003; "Plant Files: Detailed
Information on California Flannelbush, California Fremontia
(Fremontodendron californicum)," at www.davesgarden.com; Sam
W. Haynes, University of Texas at Arlington, "Manifest Destiny", at
www.pbs.org/kera/usmexicanwar/prelude/md_manifest_destiny.html;
"Frémont, John Charles", *The New Columbia Encyclopedia*, Edited
by William H. Harris and Judith S. Levey (New York and London,
Columbia University Press, 1975).

After 'The Island (with constant chaos)'
'Spirit of the Dead Watching': English translation of Paul Gauguin,
Manao tupapau, 1892, oil on burlap mounted on canvas.

ACKNOWLEDGEMENTS

Some of these poems, or earlier versions of them, have been published in the following: *Ambit, Envoi, Great Works*, www.jacksonmaclow. com, *Leviathan Quarterly, London Grip, The London Magazine, Moving Worlds, Oasis, Ninth Decade, Poetry Review, Shearsman, Staple Magazine, Tears in the Fence*, and *The Warwick Review* and also its website www2. warwick.ac.uk/fac/arts/english/writingprog/warwickreview/.

The poem-sequence 'Speak To Me Silently: Still Life and Poetry,' was published in *Long Poem Magazine* 3, 2010.

The Lascaux Variations: Fractals of Being, first published in *The Warwick Review*, was subsequently published as a limited-edition pocket portfolio, with images by John Wright, by Permanent Press, 2009.

The poems in *Leaping Down to Earth* (see Notes), with images by Stephen Chambers and Tom Hammick, were published as a limited edition by Permanent Press / Pratt Contemporary, 2008. 'After "The Island (with constant chaos)"' from that book was reprinted in *A Room to Live in: A Kettle's Yard Anthology*, edited by Tamar Yoseloff, (Cambridge: Salt Publishing, 2007).

'London Buddleia' was published in an earlier version in the anthology *Good Company*, edited by James Kissane (Grinnell, IA: Grinnell College Press, 2000).

'The Wilds of London', with images by Stephen Chambers, was published as a limited edition pamphlet by Pratt Contemporary Art, Ightham, Sevenoaks, Kent, 2006.

The following five poems were published in the Backwoods Broadsides Chaplet Series, No. 56, *Select Things*, with a drawing by Patrick Caulfield, edited by Sylvester Pollet (Ellsworth, ME, 2001): 'Dixon Enduro Pencil Sharpener,' 'Estwing Hammer,' 'Plastic in South-West Cork,' 'Plastic Potters Melamine Plate,' and 'Renault 4'.

The following poems were published in *The Guts of Shadows*, with images by John Wright, as a limited edition by Art First Contemporary Art and Permanent Press, London, 2003: 'The Approach,' 'Half Life,' 'Stairs,' 'The Repeat,' 'Song of the Cities,' 'The Convergence,' 'At the Controls,' 'Elegy for the Falling Man,' 'Cracking the Air Shell,' 'Lear in Manhattan,' and ''Music for the Retreat.' 'Song of the Cities' was reprinted in *September 11, 2001: American Writers Respond*, edited by William Heyen (Etruscan Press, Silver Springs, MD, 2002), and 'At the Controls' was reprinted in *On the Wing: American Poems of Air and Space Flight*, edited by Karen Yelena Olsen (Iowa City: University of Iowa Press, 2005).

"The Meeting" was first published in the catalogue of the exhibition of paintings by Jeremy Annear in 2004 at The New Millennium Gallery, St. Ives, Cornwall.